My Little Dysfunctional
Family Album

Sean Maher

RUNNING PRESS

PHILADELPHIA · LONDON

9 8 7 6 5 4 3 2 1

Digit on the right indicates the number of this printing
Library of Congress Control Number: 2009924761

ISBN 978-0-7624-3563-0
Cover and interior design by Jason Kayser
Edited by Jennifer Leczkowski
Special thanks to Ron Kanfi
Typography: Adobe Jenson and Pinch

Running Press Book Publishers
2300 Chestnut Street
Philadelphia, PA 19103-4371

Visit us on the web!
www.runningpress.com

Photographs

Integrity is for people
who don't know how

to work the system.

Letting the other guy
take the fall can be
a real time-saver.

Dreams are just goals
for people who are
kidding themselves.

The honor system
means free.

Clothes make the man.
Lack of clothes
make the woman.

Initiative is for suckers.

Farting in public is only
appropriate when it's done
in your brother's face.

Bad things happen to good people mainly because good people aren't as good as they think they are.

Revenge is a special kind of promise that you make to yourself.

Being a bitch is commonly mistaken for confidence.

I don't think God
is as uptight as people
make Him out to be.

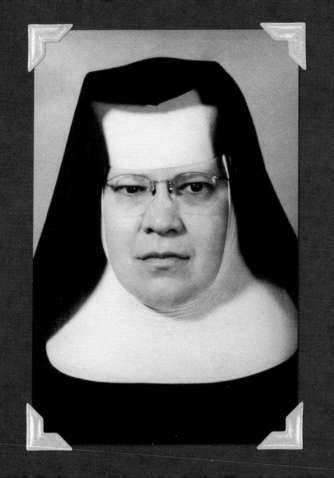

Beating a dead horse

sounds like fun.

When life hands you
lemons, chuck 'em at
the neighbor's dog.

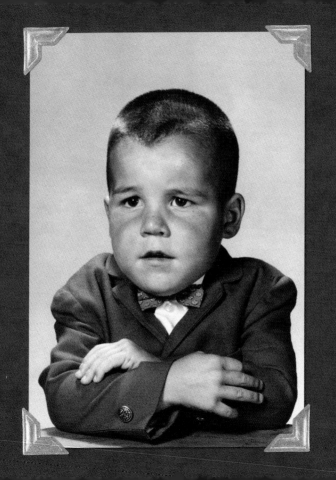

Giving in to peer pressure

is just an opportunity to be cool.

Amounting to a hill
of beans is tougher

than one might think.

Free spirit is just
a euphemism for slut.

Depression is just
your body's way
of telling you
that you're no good.

I need a restraining order

against my own demons.

I remember when stalking

was considered

romantic and cute.

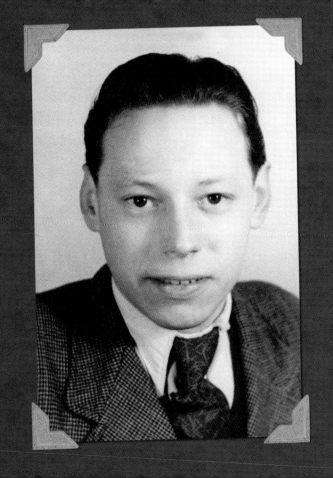

Dysfunction isn't
very Christmasy.

God should judge people
by their net worth

like we do in the real world.

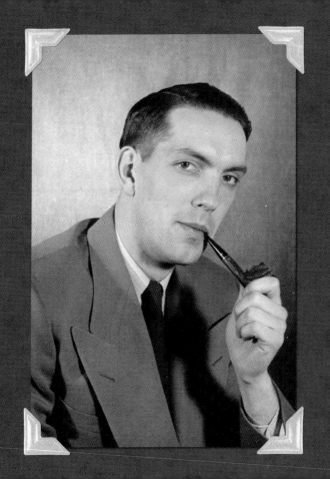

Maybe God shouldn't bless
America so much.

Wisdom is the product
of lots and lots
of really stupid mistakes.

I'm not a vegetarian,
but I want people
to think I am.

Peace has never

won a war.

It's only funny until

someone loses an eye...

and then it's
downright hilarious!

If at first you don't succeed,
pout and mope around.

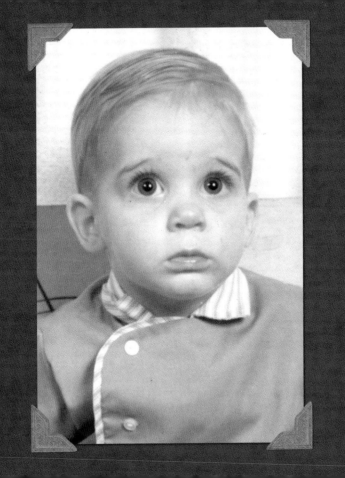

Congratulations for whatever
you think you did that
was so friggin' important.

Many people

find my creepiness

quite endearing.

I think wearing shoes

makes me appear smarter.

If I didn't have you,
the skeletons in my closet
would be the only
friends I'd have left.

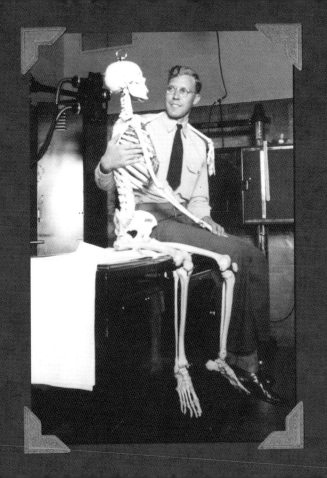

Self-confidence is just

a matter of forgetting

what a fraud you are.

Where there's a will,
there's an excuse.

My favorite egg substitute

is more bacon.

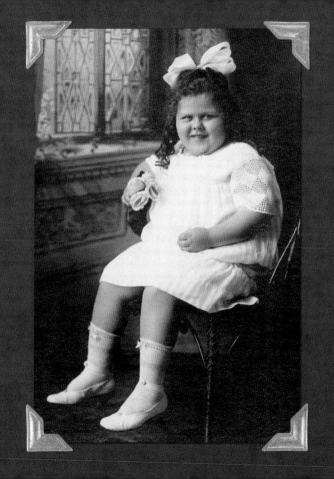

Newlyweds don't like
you to even joke
about wife-swapping.

Winners don't need

to worry about things

like sportsmanship.

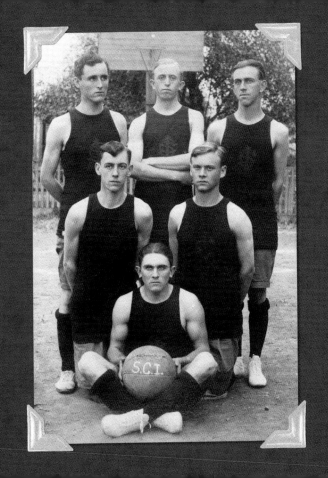

Vegetarians eventually
get hungry and fall
back in line
with the rest of us.

Eccentric is just
a sophisticated way
of saying gay.

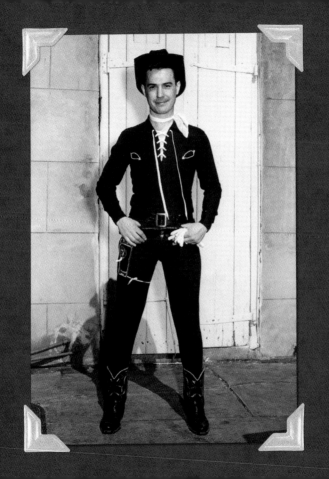

A brother is a best friend
that hits you.

Mom was right.
A father figure would have
just gotten in the way.

Maybe you should've taken better care of yourself.

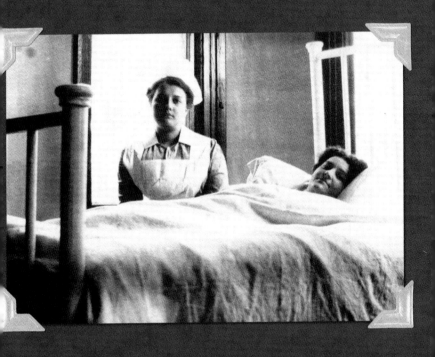

Is Heaven underground?
Because that's where they
put my Grandpa.

Looks can only get you so far, because eventually you'll have to put out.

Just look at you.

Who knew you'd blossom

into such an

awkward spaz?

Let's face it.
What does a restraining
order mean to someone
who loves you
as much as I do?

Keeping the Peace on Earth.

I bet someday they'll find
a planet out there where
everybody doesn't hate me.

Thanks for nothin'.

DNA should mind its
own business.

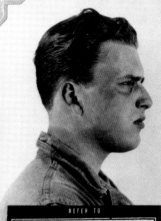

REFER TO

CII- 809,590.

BUREAU OF CRIMINAL IDENTIFICATION AND INVESTIGATION
P. O. BOX 1859, SACRAMENTO, CALIFORNIA

CALIFORNIA
YA 21455
S GASKER
JULY 2   1954

Youth is wasted on the young.

Space is wasted on the old.

Mom says the other children are just jealous

of my bed-wetting.

Medication that's not prescribed to you is the best kind.

Halloween is like

Christmas for faggots.

I still haven't figured out
how to turn
Rock 'n' Roll into poon.

Dikes don't care

to have a boy's finger

in their hole.

The bitch gene never seems
to skip a generation.

As soon as you realize
how gullible people are,
the world is your oyster
my friend.

I thought motherhood
only happened
to those bad girls.

You have a second chance
to make a first impression
if you're wearing
a good disguise.

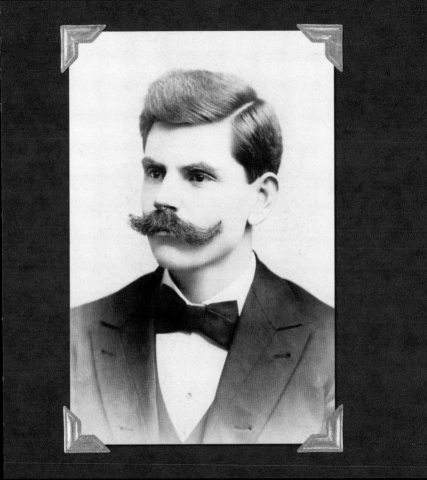

Boy crazy is just
a discrete way
of saying horny.

Lesbians are women that have never quite outgrown "Truth or Dare."

Decency is a developmental stage that we all eventually grow out of.

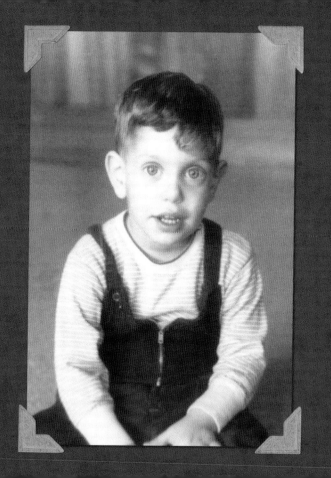

Dedication

This book is dedicated to my brothers and sisters.
Thank you for all of your support.

Mark

Julie

Terry

David

Jacqueline

and Mike

But not Kelli.
She can kiss my ass.